Dear Dad: You're Dead,
Dear Dead: You're Dad

poems, essays, and reflections from a youngest daughter

Audrey Jean

ISBN: 979-8-9893242-0-0
eISBN: 979-8-9893242-1-7
LCCN: 2024901520

Published by: Two Small Smudges

Cover Art by ThePoetDraws
Cover design by Audrey Jean
Author Photography by Paige Young / https://apaigephotography.com/
Book design and typography by Audrey Jean
Editor Sarah Knapp

Referenced works include:
Dungeons & Daddies Podcast
Spanish Sahara as performed by Foals
Innocent (Taylor's Version) as performed by Taylor Swift

This book was formatted using Adobe Jensen Pro and Perpetua fonts.

dedication

Retire, verb.
re-tire

To withdraw from action or danger; Retreat
> *("I need to retire for the night before I do something I might regret.")*
> **See also:** the crash of broken plates and spit venom at 11:30 pm night after night, hissed words carrying through the vents and into the ducts of the house

To withdraw especially for privacy
> *("Leave me alone. I don't want to—no. No, Gene, I mean it!")*
> **See also:** mother sleeping on the couch in the living room, not just because she's bone-tired every evening from carrying the weight of the family on shoulders not built to bear the brunt of this narcissistic ecosystem.

To move back: Recede
> *("Well of course you're moving back; you know you can't make it on your own.")*
> **See also:** every success attributed to home, every failure to the individual.

To go to bed
> *("Why do you always go to bed so early when you stay over?")*
> **See also:** my room has always mercifully been the one place he'd never go.

To withdraw from one's position or occupation; conclude one's working or professional career.
> *("When are you going to finally publish your book so I can retire? You know those signed copies are going to be worth something.")*
> **See also:** I can't remember the last time he's ever asked me what it is I'm writing about.

> **See also:** surprise.

dedication

I. Dear Dad: You're Dead

II. The Major Arcana

III. Dear Dead: You're Dad

I.

Dear Dad: You're Dead

rooms you might find in my father's house

Euclidean space, bigger on the inside
with monuments to John Wayne stacked
so high they blot the Son out.
    A fealty sworn to a bygone era
    of cowboys and real men and women
    who knew their place.
    Rugged individualism even when every
    character is a xeroxed copy
    of itself.
Darkened corners of white-yellow lights flickering, pallid
excuses for ambiance and color correction,
jaundiced versions of oneself tucked
like a time forgotten shrine
at the back of the house.

A bedroom littered with the detritus of sleep
attempts. Two broken scales, a dusty bipap machine,
    artificial lungs struggling
    to inflate.
    A dresser filled with clothes
    that hang off the bones
    of a man half his weight and twice his ego.
    Powdered appetite suppressants
    baked into the collars of each shirt,
        mustard yellow, ketchup red, counting
    calories on his sleeves,
whittling himself to nothing.

A Television Room to rival the Sistine Chapel;
painted *Lord of the Rings* and *Harry Potter* statues
like idols, stained glass and dusty
cobwebs, a stereo and subwoofer that
shake the whole house.

Garage like a sauna. Heated to ward
off the winter chill but never warm enough to thaw
his opinions of the holiday season

Guest bedroom with boxes fit
to bursting in the closet
of clothes he's determined he'll
fit into if only to
regress twenty more years.
This gilded room of glittering memorabilia, with a bed that's only been
slept in

by a dead man.
Ashes of my grandfather, rings from my grandmother, together
again if only by space
and time
and determination
which is more than they bothered to give each other.

And finally,
a tabletop colonized by debtor bills and collections,
paperwork for men who never got to serve
and so
make battlefields wherever
they can
even if it's only with themselves.
Final notices and past collections,
wielding the self-made swords of financial
illiteracy, come to hack at any
progress he could have possibly made under
the guise of "too good a deal
to pass up," leaving him to wonder,
at the end of every month, why he's back to
being buried
under one-dollar deals.

diet coke tastes like

Summer, 2002. 90 degrees in the shade.

"Jesus. I never should have let you mow the lawn. Look at how much
you missed—are you blind?"

> no, dad. I'm nine, and dreaming about *The Fellowship of the Ring*,
> elves and men and dwarves, heroic battles and fire-edged swords,
> of having my own room without dusty corners or shadowed edges,
> and you dressing me in anything but the khakis and polo shirt you
> bought for me

two sizes too big.
as if you could forget the number
you belittle me about.

family therapy session 1

Why don't you just tell him how you feel?

say i spit
the pain
& burden of
your desires back
to you; could
you swallow them
without complaint?

this call could not be completed as dialed

                                & if
i picked up
just   one   more
time
& you said—

& if
you called me
one last time
to say—

            & if
i saved your voicemail
from three years ago
to hear—

goodbye

                                i love you

                see you soon

family therapy session 2

if i
keep my thoughts
clutched inside my chest
do you think we can survive?
will you look back to me & say

you can see light peeking

through the cracks in my shell,

carapace shattered, &

tell me in that typical

father voice

that i have nothing

to be afraid of?

the thumbs fit weird

i am exactly 50 percent
of two people; no more,
no less. two halves of wholes
separated, slid into the
body of one who hasn't
yet learned how to wear her skin
right. like a glove two sizes
too small, or a pair of scissors
meant for the wrong hand, chafing
and clashing within, clinging tight
to the pieces of me
parsed out for themselves,
miniature reflecting pools of distorted
memories and self reflection.

the thumbs fit weird, the shoes
pinch my toes, the shirt clings to a
tummy too broad while
my pants engulf my entire lower half, drowning
me in fabric so rough i know exactly
what side of the family these genes
come from.

family therapy session 3

Childhood looks like a pillar
chipped and carved away
to resemble my father's eyes,
staring back no matter what angle
I look.

Middle school adds a second,
this pillar cinched around the center,
pulled taut with a
measuring tape cutting into the marble.

High School adds an optical illusion,
three for the price of one:
a gifted student running on fumes
a daughter determined to leave the house before the house leaves her
a young woman running from the shadows of a father
whose appearance flashes back at her from every reflective surface.

College takes a sledgehammer to the colosseum of my youth
leaving me to gasp on the ashes, lying down
to make an angel in the dust left behind.

weighed down

I used to love picking the feathers out of my parents' pillows. Beyond compulsion, or the childhood desire to see what happened, it was a way to feel as though I could do something that resulted in change. There was a finite amount of fluff inside the pillows, after all. Only so much down to go around, only so many dead birds stuffed inside the satin coverlet. I would warp and twist the pillows each, punching it between my six-year-old fists, flattening the cover taut so the feather pins would poke through the fabric, delight ripe for the picking.

One by one, I'd pull them through the fabric, snowy-white and so soft and still sharp to the touch if I put too much pressure on the tips. I'd let them float down onto the bedspread in all of their glory, the odd brown or black feather among their pale number a welcome delight. I'd building feather-castles where I sat, balancing on knobbled knees on an antique waterbed, wondering just whether the feathers might be strong enough to poke a hole through the plastic, wondering what it might look like for something so soft, tickly, and strangely weightless to have that much of an impact.

I never had the guts to see if it was possible. Instead, I'd keep my attention on my limited destruction, pulling feathers finger-hold by finger-hold until they covered the bed's surface and I contemplated what it meant to take and take and take until there was nothing more to give.

Until the pillow's insides floated on the summer air coming in from the windows, and I was left with a mess of my own curiosity, the limp, half remains of a pillow, and a wonder of just how many birds had been sacrificed for a night spent on useless, white feathers.

I still want to know what weighs more: the chance of my pulling at loose ends and feathered edges, or sitting in the aftermath of a mistake I can't put right again.

enough

when i rewrite the dictionary
i'm going to bookend this word
between "never" and
"not good;" they're too close of bedfellows
to be so far separated, and i'm too
familiar with longing for closeness,
no matter the cost or what's best,
to let them stay so
far apart.

i can't put my finger on the first time i
heard the word and felt loss so acutely that i began
to look for something that had never been mine
in the first place. if i tried, i'm sure my heart
could wind back the clock,
warp the timeline to show a father
with glazed anger dripping when his daughter
couldn't fit into the corduroy pants he'd picked out without
bothering to check if they might fit her
or not.

maybe my heart would show me a girl
barely in her maturity, pinching parts of her body
between her fingers and wondering
how she can be accused of equally having too much
and too little. she's not even sure what *enough* means,
only that her father says it's something she isn't.
perhaps she's still so young as to be unaware of the
"enough" shaped hole
where her left ventricle should be, the gaping space that struggles
to find something—
anything—
to fill it.

time will age her, will lead her
to men and women whose square edges
scrape the tender round hole of her heart,
their jagged sides and sharp
corners will cut the scar tissue that's barely healed from the last
intruder before realizing no matter
how hard they shove, they just don't want the
bloody pulp of a girl left
in the wake of their violence.

who needs a 401k?

if   i   had
a   penny
for   every   measure
i   could   never
      meet

an ingredients family

1. Preheat the oven, the one that takes so long to get to temperature that you might as well turn it on earlier that day; make sure to plan ahead just enough to absolve you of any future mistakes. Never mind the carbon monoxide filling your house.
Don't be a baby; you know you can't trust what you hear in the news.

2. Get the mixing bowl—the one given to you from your grandmother, given to her by her mother, a line of matriarchs standing in the same shoes you claim pinch your toes.

Next the mixing spoon, the one whose wood is chipped like teeth, hewn from each sharpened gaze leveled on you the last time you asked the family recipes to be written down. As though tradition could bear the pain of being spilled in ink.
Stop asking for them and listen instead. Memorize my words.

3. Combine in the first bowl: eggs and sugar, room temperature butter.

No, not melted.
Did I say melted?

4. Beat. Beat until the mix is light like fluffy clouds, like dreams of what we might become when our aspirations are allowed to flourish. Beat until the mix is as effortless as the way you remember your mother was as she floated around the house, as though she hadn't worked a sixty-hour work week. Beat until it's as liminal as the smile your grandmother once gave you when you got all As on your report card. Watch sugar and fat melt together; look how they withstand the pressure and pain to become something beautiful.
Why haven't you?

5. Incorporate a healthy glug of vanilla, let it coat the back of your spoon before you beat it in with the rest. Smell that? That's what keeping your head down and your mouth shut smells like. That's what dinner on the table after ten hours of thankless labor, of dishes and mending and turning a blind eye, smells like.
That's what your great-grandmother smelled like; the good vanilla.

6. Combine the dry ingredients: flour, baking powder, salt. Not that much salt—you want it sweet, don't you?
Don't ask me why just fucking do it.

7. Assess. Is your batter too dry? Add some milk, some extra fat never hurt anyone so long as you know it's not for you, so long as you know the best way to disguise it, to dress and redress and layer until your belly lies smoothly beneath your layers.

Too wet? You didn't measure right, then.
I really don't understand what's so hard. Can't you follow instructions?

8. Bake.
Don't ask me how long; you'll know when it's done. You'll know it by the smell, by the way the surface springs back to the touch. Stop complaining about the pain; your burned fingertips are an earned badge; means you're part of the family.

typical fat girl problems

There's only one diet for me
& that's the brat diet.
I want to calm the anxiety in my stomach
by being given what I want, when I want it.
I want affirmations that I'm a good girl until I gag
on my own self-confidence.
Nothing tastes as good as validation feels, & when
I'm slipping into the sheets of my bed at night,
I fantasize about being kissed on the forehead, tucked in, &
told I've been the best daughter a family could ask for.

I wasn't born into a family that believed in raising brats,
but dammit wouldn't that have been nice?

the nature of healing

Of all the curses I've tasted, I still believe healing is the dirtiest word there is. I know I've spit vitriol, used every c, s, f, t, buy a vowel, guess a consonant, dirty word there is. I'd like to solve the riddle, Pat. Healing feels like giving up, surrendering to the Atlas-sized realization that years of muscle-building and back breaking do not, in fact, make me a Mythical Figure, but fucking tired[1].

Healing builds character, placed and nailed down like the boards of Thesus's ship. First, fingerprints worn away and replaced, next the rotting liver, pancreas, and intestines removed once they interfere with my work, scraped edges scarred from rusty scalpels and saws, until — is that still me, standing there?

Can a replica know it's only been created to stand in for something it will never be? Healing is looking at the *Mona Lisa*, *Scream*, at *Sunflowers* and *Water Lilies* and wondering how it might feel to be printed in facsimile of perfection, knowing your paper was formed with the earth's dying breath.

Healing feels like 40 hours of work and mandated OT, sent down the line with a rictus grin that says, "This is good for you. Self-work builds character."

Healing means going slow and telling yourself to be happy with a participation trophy while the award-givers post about it on your friend's social media sites. Congratulations, you did it. But don't forget that while you were bent over double and crying in agony, while you where white-knuckling it down that last turn, when all the fans had left and gone home for the day, they created a highlight reel of everyone who passed you by unencumbered, uncaring, and unwilling to pay attention to anything else.

Healing is digging my fingers into the muck beneath me, pressing dirt and beetles and worms into my palms to form a paste with which I might patch myself together. That I might grind the earth's marrow into a bloody cast of regeneration, feeding off the energy of that which crawled beneath me. I am a <u>mud-woman, wh</u>ose features I am carving, hollowing with uncertain fingers,

1   fucking fight me, Sisyphus

piecing together to create something whole. Healing is going back to slice off what I believe doesn't serve me until I look in the mirror and see only my eyes, my nose, my full mouth. Would that I could simply baptize myself in the salt tears that make the mud slick, running rivulets of agony and exhaustion.

Healing is looking at this woman's reflection and introducing myself to a green-eyed girl who doesn't think her full cheeks or sloping nose looks like a poor man's caricature of her father, or the fathers who came before.

Healing is searching for the pieces of my grandmother's grandmother, to thank the resiliency of the women that came before, those whose hunched shoulders I've found myself growing into, whose saddened gaze tells me they will *always want more for me* when I inevitably find parts of my father hiding in my features again and again and again.

Healing is learning to can and preserve the tears that made a muddy mess of me, to patch myself back together with the salt water I now call holy, consecrating it so that I might anoint every part of my body with the pain that brought me here.

Healing is believing that sanctification of that pain will be enough to give me purpose, only to find joy in the (re)making.

limboing my way to hell

Go low.
I said low.
L o w e r.

Why are you *proud* of that number?

> Have you ever wondered what it might've felt like
> to gorge yourself on affection?
> How selfless love and support might soothe your
> belly in a way twenty pounds off at the scale
> never could?

clay roots

I really thought once that outgrowing you would be the only way to shut you up. That I'd made peace with the idea that when you saw me you only ever saw your greatest failures staring you back in the face.

Not that you'd admit to knowing what failure tastes like; for someone who mocks the abused and taken advantage of, who says those who were foolish enough to be taken in by false promises deserve the pain, you sure were the victim in every chapter in your story. I thought I'd shed your vitriol like old skin, slithered on my belly away from the dead shell of disappointment and misplaced trust that you'd love me regardless of who I was. I thought I'd forget the sound of fury, the suggestions that I could be anyone's kid but yours, and replace them with words of affirmation from when I was young.

But it turns out those don't exist, either.

I thought I'd outgrow the feeling of being looked at in disappointment, but that weight has a gravity all its own every morning I push myself out of bed.

Do you understand how hard I've tried to forget the times you said you wanted to throw me away? All after those afternoons you'd worked so hard to sculpt me in your image, but found the clay of my foundation wouldn't yield, no matter how many times you pressed at my soft pockets of insecurity.

I've never been the forgetting sort when it comes to a grudge.

I wonder who I learned that from.

hanna lake dr

When I say I want to go home
    what I mean is take me back.
    Back to when safety meant
    sleeping in my mother's arms,
    and hiding the curves of my tummy
    in oversized dresses so I could
    keep pretending to be royalty.
What I mean is let me go
    to the spot where my childhood once stood,
    where we walked through the backyard
    picking pinky-size, sugar-sweet wild strawberries.
    Where my swing set would launch me
    into the sky, and where my sister told
    me to play a CD on repeat for her cat
    while she was gone
    with her dad for the weekend.
Bring me to the overgrown grass and broken cement of what was
    once a home and let me root through the rubble
    to find some fragment of when we were happy.

Or did the construction company take that
    too?

don't touch

plastic wrap surrounds
the ocean that is my
girlhood imagination,
daydreams and half-awake
fantasies of barbie dolls dressed
like audrey hepburn and rex harrison,
figurines of poorly tempered
three-headed dogs and wizards with fragile
broomsticks clutched between china-fine fingers,
porcelain ballerinas fit to dance and
dangle on the limbs of an
evergreen, gold plated collectable
cards meant to be "*displayed*
only, audrey. don't rip the packaging
or they'll be useless."

hours i'll never get back spent
circling the mcdonald's drive-thrus, requests for a
happy meal toy that will never know the taste
of oxygen, the both of us deprived of
the freedom we really want.

one day I'll remind him that "no" is a complete sentence

The times I've tried to say "no" stack like the boxes piled in my father's house on garage sale day.
>(two for a dollar, or best offer, hauled out into the Michigan sun to yellow like the grass.)

No, I don't want to hock thirty years of Western memorabilia with its horses staring wide-eyed and petrified at the onlookers.
>(what must it feel like to run and run and run and still be the target of wandering eyes?)

No, I don't want to talk to the men from the Masonic temple who he snidely reminds me he sees more often than he does me.
>(funny, since he's happy to pay the dues to meet with them but says he's running low when child support comes around.)

No, I don't want to sit and listen to WLAV bad-talk the governor, or pay attention to the Hillary memes ripped from the Facebook pages of those same Masonic members.
>(why do they keep looking at me like I'm built of second-wife material?)

I'm twenty-six, college-educated, and still this one syllable is the only one I can't say.
>(not to him.)

all my least favorite words start with *d*

I was 11 when I tried to divine the
reason I didn't have friends the same
size as me with which to swap clothes.
Pulled card after card,
boxed set from the local Barnes & Noble,
beginners deck and *guide to tarot*,
all to try and discover the reason my sister
wouldn't let me hang out with her
and her friends when they would come over — why
she decided to stay at their house and not ours.
I ripped pages from the booklet to
look at them all at once,
manifesting answers and
how-tos to make my
hair blonde, my eyes
less muddy, my jeans fit the way
my dad wanted them to —
right at the hips instead of
pulled over my tummy.

I drew purple-backed cards until
I thought my fingers might bleed dry from
paper cuts, hoping they might
have the answers to why mom never came home
in a good mood anymore,
why we'd had to mandate
food only at breakfast, lunch, and dinner,
no after school, late night, or after dinner
snacks. All the while my body starved
for something that couldn't be put
on a plate.

Each overly laminated face glared up at me, reversed
or head-on, flipped with clear
or muddy intentions,
as though to ask
whether i really
needed them
to spell it
out for
me.

("If you're such a smart girl, why don't you fucking act like it?")

dear dad: you're dead

your last sentence
stumbles, an old refrain
in the space between my ears
the day before your
thin lips choked on your last breath.
and still you pull me until I
unravel, strand by strand.
you continue to speak
even though you've since used all the
oxygen in the room,
last words like ash,
rasped promises that will never
be kept, withheld assurances of pride
three steps out of reach, long strides
I will never catch up with
even now that age has hobbled
and bent you over
double.

horror movie houses

It's 2004, and fear is on the menu.
    fingers prying at the tendons and ligaments
    of a long rotted marriage, bones creaking
    from standing with only
    one leg, the other devoured and left to rot in the
    therapist's office I'm dragged into
    every other Tuesday.

It's 2004, and my family croaks,
    swallows tongue and reason in a black water bath of
    half-truths and fuller lies, fattened like cows
    to slaughter, led by hook or by crook
    to the judge's stand, called
    to face the grotesque creature
    twelve-years, five-months, and twenty-two days
    has turned them into.

It's 2004, and all feelings are packed into
    air-tight boxes, relocated to the attic
    of two failed marriages prior—
    what strange bedfellows are these?
    They stack so neatly, trauma—
    packed & unpacked & packed again.

It's 2004, and I don't know if I like how this house
    creaks and shimmies in the wind. How it
    breathes like it's got something to say. Like
    the walls have their own opinions painted into
    the drywall, which swell and seethe
    with every whisper we share.

i learned about cannibalism at the 11am mass at Holy Family Catholic Church

We always sat at the back of the congregation, even if my mother hated it, her furtive glances at my father as we stepped in mid-opening chorus. 11:10 or so. If you have to be fashionably late for something, well then my father figured he might as well make it church. To him, we were only going for the coffee and donuts and so he could bring it up as a way that he was "trying" in couple's counseling years down the road.

Sitting in the back felt like watching reruns of Family Court on a Tuesday morning. It's not quite relaxing enough to doze off with the up down up down up down aerobics class built into every hour-long sermon, but not nearly engaging or compelling or even vaguely interesting enough for a seven-year-old obsessed with Sailor Moon and sleepy Sunday mornings. Out of the corner of her eye, I could feel my mother shooting me less than enthused looks when I'd ruffle the hymnal pages too loudly, or poke my father in the side to keep him from falling asleep. Her impatience had reached its peak with him, but I was steadily getting closer to the very top.

I thought I was doing the world a service; no one had to hear him snore this way, but his grunts of displeasure and her venomous looks of disbelief were the all too familiar undercurrent to the lecture from the front of the room. I wanted him awake, anyway. Wanted him to crack jokes with me, to at least help pass the time, desperate for some sort of connection beyond the glazed-eye stupor sitting in an overheated, packed church will put you in when you're too old to stay in the playroom with the other children.

I never got to ask if he felt his nonchalance and half-asleep stupor was some sort of "fuck you" to the Lutheranism he claimed to believe in, generational tablespoons rebuttals, refusals, and theses of why this religion wasn't his own, even if his parents had force fed him spoonful by spoonful their own variation.

I would be nearly crawling out of my skin by the time communion came around, watching my mother leave to go line up with the other baptized participants, over 80 percent of the congregation queueing to get up, to get it over with, and come back.

This would leave my father and I in the exclusive "outsiders" club, ten to twenty or so strong, leaning back in the pews as the shepherded remainders lined up to take their daily bread.

"You know." My father leaned in closer, listerine and old spice and aftershave strong enough to break through the incense and old people musk. My ears pricked up, desperate for the attention, dying to know what was so secretive that he couldn't outright say it. **"If they eat the Body of Christ and drink his blood, that makes them all cannibals."**

He winked, a secret we were supposed to share, before righting himself in the pew, a hearty, huffing laugh under his breath seconds before my mother returned, the red rims of her eyes zeroing in on the way my mouth opened to bleat: **"Mommy. Dad says you're a cannibal."**

He really should've known a seven-year-old has no volume control, especially not in the aftermath of post-communion prayer.

We weren't allowed to sit next to each other after that, and under no circumstances was I ever to repeat his little joke to my grandmother.

the only time lying is considered not only acceptable, but expected.

Eulogy for my father given January, 2020

Hello everyone and thank you so much for coming. My name, for those of you who I may not have gotten a chance to introduce myself to, is Audrey. I'm Gene's youngest daughter. Thank you all so much for coming and being here with us today to celebrate my father; your being here and support means a great deal.

When I was in college, and starving for anything but dorm food, Dad took me out for dinner to one of our favorite Chinese restaurants. When ordering his favorite, he asked the waiter that the wonton soup not be made "too heavy."

"You know, *one-ton*. Don't make it too heavy on yourself; you're a strong guy, but you shouldn't pick up one-ton without stretching."

The waiter smiled, though his expression was confused, and dipped out to place our order in with the kitchen.

Sure enough, while my egg drop soup was brought out perfectly, dad's wonton soup was brought out as just broth, some veggies, and no "one-ton" wonton.

He giggled about that on his best, and worst, of days.

While reflecting on how in the heck to even begin discussing my father's life, I dug deep, and found that some of the best parts of who I am are part of me courtesy of my father. Mainly, I've reflected that, just like dad, I enjoy talking the most.

You've all met Gene, so I trust that you know he was a talker, too; I've never known him to go into a room and not make at least one friend, and possibly get into at least one near-argument with someone else. He was passionate, and strong willed about what he cared about, two more traits that I have been fortunate to inherit, and Dad cared about a whole lot. He cared about his family, he valued his community and giving back. He cared about his country, there's never been any doubt about that.

His passion and dedication translated into the man we all saw and connected with; his zeal and enthusiasm resonated, and he had a charisma that, even if you didn't see eye to eye with him, you couldn't help but engage for want of conversation.

In the days following the announcement of dad's passing, my family and I have received nothing but outpourings of support, of love and sympathy; I've seen fond memories of time spent talking with dad, exchanged pictures of sunsets and sunrises, examples of his dedication to the Masons and Knights Templar, to his neighbors. It's truly humbling to know that the man who'd picked me up in his arms so easily when I was little, who'd taught me as best he could how to mow the lawn (even if I couldn't keep my lines straight), who'd spent countless hours watching, rewatching, and dissecting the Harry Potter movies, books, and collecting memorabilia, was so well loved, so well regarded and respected. To know that he has such a lasting impact, left such a profound mark in so many people's lives, is as much as I could ever ask for as his daughter.

Irvin Yalom, an American psychologist who studies existentialism, pondered the realities of one's death. Yalom concludes that we only truly die when the last person who has known us, who remembers us, passes on, and takes their memory of the departed with them. I've found great comfort in knowing that, through all of you, through our collective memories, and experiences, through the many lives that my father was able to impact and influence, he's not gone, but still very much with us.

Even as we say goodbye for now, I am comforted by the laughter inspired by his never-ending dad jokes, the strength of his bear hugs as he held me close, the scratch of his beard when he kissed my cheek to tell me he loved me. The sound of his voice when he'd leave a message just to talk, to check how I was doing, wanting to make sure that I wasn't just working to work, but getting out and living my life, as well. These are the memories that I will hold the closest, treasure even when the grief threatens to suffocate and crush all happiness from my day. This is the way I will honor him and keep him, ever present, with me.

Thank you all so much for coming and celebrating his life with us, for keeping my father alive in your memories, your stories, and your hearts. It is because of your collective support and sympathy, that I don't feel as though I've lost my father, but rather gained a greater knowledge and proof of the life he lived: passionate, proud, deeply caring, and with the slightest twist of humor.

death doesn't mean you got away with it, just that i have to be nice

The eulogy I never gave

Thank you all for coming; for those who haven't rubbernecked at the twenty-something trying to keep her shit together, I'm Gene's daughter. He might have told you about me before, my name's The Liberal One.

I was the one ruined by going to school, even though he'll tell you all the time it was his idea to push me to go, anyway, and then called me complaining when I didn't have enough money to drive down to see him. When I was in college, he'd call me weekly to check on how my grades were going, which was more or less a thinly veiled threat that if I didn't work harder that I'd never amount to anything.

And when I did call him to say I'd aced a test, that I'd worked to improve my GPA, or hey I'd decided to change my major to something that didn't make me want to end myself, he'd ask why I thought that would matter?

He knew I was going to succeed, after all, even if he didn't share that sentiment with me. I was his daughter, and no daughter of his was going to fail anything. (At least, this was before I took a sociology class and started really questioning his authority. No daughter of his would dare ever do that.

Before I took a class on women's politics and social justice and told him that his privilege meant that even though he struggled, he had no idea what it meant to be anything but white.

Before I voted for the very first time and told him, when he demanded to know how I could've betrayed him, that I could never in good faith vote for a Republican.
No daughter of his would ever do that.

That probably sounds familiar; those of you that knew my father knew he loved to talk politics, loved to know how you could possibly think he could ever be wrong, and if you got along with him, oh boy did he have so many supposed news articles to show you to validate his opinions.

And if you didn't, well, you'd see them anyway.)

But that's not the dad I remember best. The father that, despite his claims of being uncertain, raised me and brought me into this world. My father baked cakes for his daughter's birthday—as long as they were what he wanted or was in the mood for. And he took us to the Harry Potter movies, buying paraphernalia enough to sink our family into so much debt my mother's credit score took over a decade to recover after they'd divorced. They weren't toys for me to play with, but investments in a future that he was certain we'd find a way to have together—whether anyone else wanted it or not. They weren't meant to be used, they—like the women in his life—were meant to be looked at, owned but never allowed to fulfill a greater purpose. Kept on a shelf and blamed for not being worth enough when they didn't pay off in his greater vision of things.

He was the type of father to buy the McDonald's toys when we went through the drive-thru if only because *they'd be worth something* in the end, making his six-year-old daughter hold onto it without ripping it open. Looking, but never touching.

He was my introduction to Star Trek and Star Wars, because once he had the television on you just had to listen to his surround sound and no you weren't allowed to touch the remote.

He was even my introduction to words no white man, woman, or child should ever use; Gene never met a racial slur he didn't have to taste on his tongue to see what the fuss was about.

No, the father I knew taught me what it meant to show someone your middle finger when I mouthed off to him, put me on a diet of oatmeal and egg-whites at age nine because I looked "lumpy" in my sweatpants, and walked me around the house in tears in front of my sister and mother when I disobeyed him.
A family man, through and through; that was the father I knew.

He guided me through so many firsts. I learned at least ten new words for fat when out clothes shopping with him, experienced my first heartbreak coming home to find our family cats had been given away, and learned how to starve myself of affection so it could never be taken away or used against me.

Now, he might not have known better as we grew older; he lived year after year in tandem with my own, and we butt heads over politics that benefited him even if he couldn't see it. He only knew what was taught to him by his own father— that anger and aggression and being the loudest meant you were winning some fucked up, made-up game between the two of you, and I think if he would've had the chance to get out from under that, he might've stood a chance developing the relationship he clearly wanted to have.

Or maybe if he'd given therapy a chance beyond deciding there was nothing in him that needed fixing. Who's to say.

Thank you for coming today to share your stories of the times he made you too uncomfortable you didn't dare say anything, thank you for sharing in our grief even if you don't want to admit that it's tinted, perhaps, with the barest hint of relief.

Thank you for witnessing the required funeral pleasantries, for shaking our hands, giving hugs, and watching as I shake the yoke of disappointment off my shoulders for one final time.

sexuality

"Anyone else, but not you."
any *other* family, but not ours.
"I'll kill you." she makes promises
with more than just words,
knife-sharp smiles, sinew deep,
eyes gleaming,
dareing me to say something.
already creating a grocery list of the ways
in which I aspire to let her down.

reaches out with lukewarm fingers
to twist me round and hold me tight.
I wonder if she can feel
my traitor heart already
screaming to save the guilty vessel;
I'm running out of fingers to plug up the holes
in my sinking ship.

it takes nine more years and three Sam Adams clutched in
shaking hands before I choke
on the truth to my sister.
her eyes grow steely, her hands steady,
setting that night's dinner on the table:
"don't tell mom."
as if I need the reminder.

dirty talk

Sure, I like dirty talk.
Can we start slow?
It's been a little while
for me, I mean.

"I know you did your best."

"You handled yourself with grace."

"You did a great job."

"I could hear you talk about that for hours."

"It's okay to rest."

"I hear what you're saying."

"It's going to be okay."

"I support you and your decisions."

"I believe in you."

"I'm proud of you."

Was it good for you?

reflections on "dirty talk"

I really hate the term Daddy Issues. Let's be real: having a father, or lack thereof, doesn't mean you automatically have "Daddy Issues." What about "sperm donor who didn't know what praise meant if it wasn't directed at him" issues? Or "parent who is an absentee in everything except criticism" issues?

Why do we give our fathers all the (dis)credit? Maybe I gave myself the issues all on my own.

Maybe it's, "expectations are through the roof for matters that are out of your control" issues? Or hell, let's start to call them, "fictional fathers should come with a warning tag for getting your hopes up" issues. There's a nice ring to, "the father figure you wanted only aired on Mondays, Wednesdays, and Fridays from 3:30 to 5pm Eastern Standard Time" issues.

I'll never understand the obsession with saying that girls who don't have reliable fathers, who don't have "good" fathers, or whose fathers aren't present, have daddy issues, when really the issues are that the father figures in our lives failed us and we were never given the tools or the chance to be our own father figure. It's not an issue with a solution, it's not a problem that we created. It's a hole where a hug ought to be, a constantly chased silhouette where a pat on the back or a word of praise should be. It's watching every shadow be split into two, watching a mother take on a coat two-sizes too big where a father's arms should fit.

But we're told we have Daddy Issues as though it's our hands that slipped the jacket onto our mother's shoulders. As if we're meant to know the difference between when a smile means *come closer* or *run* when we can't even see the face it belongs to.

II.

The Major Arcana

spread for determining when the divorce will finally happen

Use this when the arguing gets too loud,
when the walls start to pull in towards you
if only to get away from the violence threatened below.
Use this to determine how many more
sleepless nights you'll have to endure
before the judge makes up their
goddamn mind.

1. DIVINATION: Will my father break more than just a plate this time?
2. THE PAST: Ancient wounds that will be rehashed whenever my mother's name is brought up in polite conversation.
3. THE HOME: A not-so certain future in a house built for a family that no longer exists.
4. THE FUTURE: How to look someone in the eye when they tell you that you're the cause of their suicidal ideation.
5. THE TRUTH: What to do with ten years of repressed anger and resentment when it bubbles into a confession of infidelity.

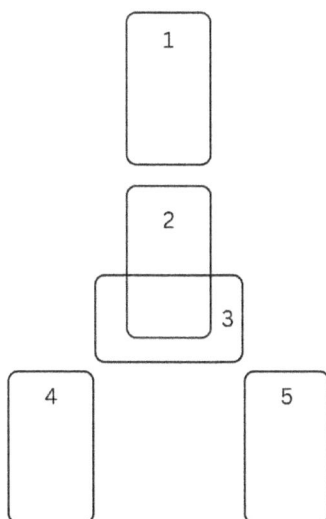

major arcana: the tower

who taught you what the tops of the trees looked like? or what it meant to breathe air hundreds of feet above, so fresh and crisp that it doesn't feel like it belongs on this planet? to keep yourself above the forest, watching silver-linings go gunmetal?

who taught you that peeking your head out the window would mean you'd have to look down, would mean you'd have to bend, would mean you'd start to fall— or jump—would mean you'd break your neck, your back, your temple—?

who taught you to speak in tongues so dangerous not even babylon could record them? words so strong they plate armor and swords and crowns, sharp enough to cut without hesitation, dragged through blood that looks like your own?

who taught you there were rocks waiting for you with open-mouthed arrogance at the bottom? gaping emptiness at the end of the world, ready to swallow you whole?

who taught you that lightning only needs to strike once before it makes its home, burrows itself so deep your every cell stands on edge?

who gave you the mud-stained glasses you swear are clear, and told you the world will never understand the way you see it?

major arcana: the moon

What would it mean to sleep without your name tucked between my back teeth?
        molars ground to dust with the memories of hellish shouting matches.

What would it mean to sleep spread out in bed?
        tucking myself under the blankets to keep you from seeing.

What would it mean to sleep a whole night through?
        scratching at a wound that refuses to seal shut, your voice echoing in
        the cavern of days between losing and no longer needing you.

What would it mean to sleep without fear burrowing through my ribcage?
        shadows creep from every corner of the room, dragged inch by inch
        closer with the falling of my eyelids, soldiers abandoning their post.

major arcana: strength

Pride: A group of lions, strength in numbers and claws like iron. Golden coated, Kings and Queens of the jungle, family means everything and one cannot exist without the rest. Even if the women work ceaselessly, breaking their backs to feed the patriarch, whose gorgeous mane means little if there's not food enough to go around, whose vainglorious destiny is to take and take and take in the name of offering protection.

Pride: to embrace who you are, to stand tall and smile - not because you must, but because you can. To look the world in the eyes and proclaim yourself fit. Satisfied. Enough.
    See also: Courage
    See also: thirty-two years in the making and I'm just beginning to get it. Sort of.

Pride: the gleam in my mother's eyes when I told her I was coming home, soon to reduce hours of driving with minutes and day-to-day phone calls. The smile on my sister's face when I told her I loved her, ran my fingers down the gnarled edges of our sisterhood—shared mothers, shared wombs—and felt the scars begin to heal.
    See also: Those damn Daddy Issues.
    See also: missing core memories of father-daughter dances, of milestone events met only with an exasperated, "well, now what are you doing?"

Pride: Living for those who accept you at your fullest, allow you to take up as much space as you need, knowing it's not a matter of being enough to go around, but that it's possible to exist together.
    See also: it's not living a lie if the lie keeps you living
    See also: I'm not saying he has anger issues, but my daddy just bought a gun and the year is 2016.

Pride: A male lion may roar the loudest, but it's the silent, clawed feet of the hunting party that spells doom across the Savannah.

spread for determining how young is too young to develop body dysmorphia

Sure, you're a kid now, but the habits
you begin will only manifest further the older
you become. Might as well get used to
the taste of disappointment; I promise you'll learn how
to spread that shit on everything.

1. GUIDANCE: For advice on how to read the glares your father shoots your way when you ask him why he gets dessert, but you don't.
2. HABIT FORMING: How long it will take for you to get used to eating plain oatmeal and egg-whites for breakfast in the morning because you need to lose 10 pounds before you start 4th grade.
3. MONEY: The best way to learn how to clip coupons so you make the most out of the buy-two-get-three-free deal at the local Arby's knowing that you'll be chastised for eating the one that's given to you.
4. REFLECTION: Wondering whether the full-sized mirror in your parents room is set up to distort the space around your stomach, cheeks, and thighs, or if your body wasn't meant to try and fit in jeans that hang this low.
5. LIFE CYCLES: The best way to handle starting your period early before you've hit double-digits, and why your body hurts so badly you don't think you can get out of bed in the morning.
6. NUTRITION: Why the only soda that you're allowed to drink begins with a *diet*.

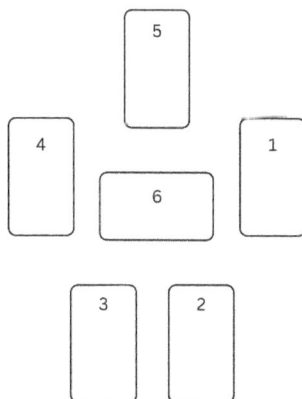

```
              ┌─────┐
              │  5  │
              │     │
  ┌─────┐     └─────┘     ┌─────┐
  │  4  │                 │  1  │
  │     │  ┌─────┐        │     │
  │     │  │  6  │        │     │
  └─────┘  └─────┘        └─────┘

       ┌─────┐  ┌─────┐
       │  3  │  │  2  │
       │     │  │     │
       └─────┘  └─────┘
```

major arcana: the empress

Pessimism is strong in my family. My mother has it, my sister has it. I have it.
Our sigil is that of a woman hunched over an endless bounty of dirty dishes,
glass of vodka,
paneless windows,
 a clock behind her that never moves.
Our words are, "Life is shit, work harder" and our matriarchal keep has been
built on the backs of women strong enough to do the work of two, yet too
burdened to bring to light how fucked the situation is.
Negative Nancy got in a drinking competition with Pessimistic Patricia and got
sent to the hospital for alcohol poisoning,
while my mother popped two advil,
rolled up her sleeves,
and clocked back in.
There are bills to pay, don't talk to me.
We chase Xanax with lies about feeling fine to silence the voice saying we're
too tired
and too spent to think, let alone go on with the
endless charade of the grind.
We aim so high that even when we miss, the stars have yet to catch up.
Aspirations greater than probability or possibility, yet we jump
and jump
and jump anyway.
My stature may be a handicap,
but it's my self-doubt that cuts my legs off at the knees
and bids me
bloody and gasping
to run the marathon of life.
Crippled and cringing, I wobble along anyway.

major arcana: the emperor

or, in 2020, 69% of the Americans who died by suicide were white males

It's a starring role.   First name on the bill,
titular character   with all the best lines.
                      You've never heard them delivered like this.
The prestige, the attention
and power.
Center stage, full lights—
don't worry if you can't remember
your lines.
                      You're a natural. It'll come to you.

Have some
      attention   affection   anger
it's all for you, baby!
Everyone here?   *They're here for you,*
      don't forget that. don't let them forget that.
pivot
keep 'em laughing
crying
cursing
keep ~~complainingtalkingexplaining~~
they could never know
unless you tell them.
you're the star,   *they're your chorus.*
You're the event,   *they're the causation,*
remember?
how did it begin?
tell us
                *tellustellus**tellus***
make them listen,
make them pay
You're the star, babe.

spread for finding a man who doesn't remind me of my father, grandfather, great-grandfather—

Use this to divine the answers to your questions
& to ensure that you don't end up
like the rest of the women
in your family.

1. INTUITION: Do you find the hairs stand up on the back of your neck from excitement, or in anticipation of needing to find the nearest exit?
2. CONVERSATION: What does it mean that he signs off every conversation with a threat of returning to the same topic later, and that he'll remember the inflections when you asked to change the subject?
3. IMAGINATION: When he looks at you, is he imagining you on his arm, or ten pounds lighter?
4. LOVE: What do you do when he insists cooking is his love language, but you find yourself going to bed after begging for scraps?
5. MARRIAGE: When he asks about your feelings about marriage, what does it mean that instead of sincerity you see an open bear trap, rusty teeth bared and well-oiled hinges waiting?
6. DECEPTION: What should you think when he knows the perfect shade and application of foundation that will cover up blemishes and merlot-colored bruises alike?

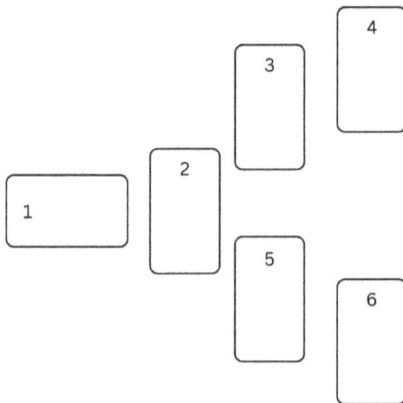

major arcana: judgment

are
you
really
gonna
eat
all
that

you
sure
you
want
to
do
that

why
would
you
say
that

are
you
gonna
make
me
repeat
myself
don'tmakehimsayitagaindon'tmakehimsayitagaindon'tm
akehimsayitagaindon'tmakehimsayitagaindon'tmakehim

major arcana: the hanged man

it's all gone tits up, hasn't it?
off the rails, up shit's creek
without a paddle. to hell
in a handbasket you've woven yourself. three
sheets to the moon.

it's time to bite the bullet,
to face the music, to meet
your maker. i've a sinking
feeling this isn't
just you crying
over spilled milk, not
when the world's balance, its last
leg to stand
on, is hanging
by a thread.

Have I sufficiently put words
to your trauma, yet?

major arcana: the wheel of fortune

stacked in my sink, the forgotten soldiers from three meals demand my blood. greatest-generation-born bowls with crusted flour and buttermilk lay bereft in a sink of soap scum and empty promises about tomorrow and tomorrow and tomorrow. pans with blackened-edges from too-well-seared chicken, the white meat so lean it was without any fat to soften the blow. sharpened knives in garish colors, as though the rainbow can distract from their purpose — Pride now available pre-sharpened for what's to come, ready to crush, score, filet, break down, slice & dice. each bloodstained, carrots, steak, beets, garlic skins still sticking, peeling like sunburn and crying for a bath.

now, they point in my direction, bay-scented hounds tasting anxiety over the stench of a clogged sink drain, fire alarm bells detecting depression, as spoons, forks, plates, graters, mugs ("you got this boss bitch" scraped into the ether) join their ranks. an army not of my design, but my forgetfulness. intention may not have created them, but damn does neglect have a funny way of bringing everyone to the table. who knew the sink would be the fertile soil required to pull a coup of this magnitude together. this woman's work is never done, and it seems they've come to make me pay for it.

these soldiers are sticky-putty-fused with flour-based glue from half-baked plans, grafted metal and ceramic and kitchen blade together. chicken-bone-fingers and pasta-sauce-stained-boots and cheese-carved mouths of despair, reeking of an unholy trinity and my failed attempts at a dinner party. they rise above my body and demand to see the supposed antique trauma, the imprinted doubt and self-loathing like china roses on my bones, gilded failure grafted into my brain, my bloodstream a cycle of defeatist language. cut me open, expose the marrow, and examine the growing cancer in the corner of my heart, the one that sounds like my grandma's laughter and smells like my father's aftershave.

major arcana: death

How fine Death looks on his pale horse, how regal. How mighty, a harbinger of the end, riding a King's stallion yet dressed in the worn cloak of the common. I imagine it's to insinuate that in the end, Death comes for all of us. That no one can escape the inevitability of time and mortality. That though it's been attempted countless times, you cannot cheat Death.

(How do I know? I've seen my father try. Time and time again, watched as his number was called and yet he refused to go. Too much to do, vastly too self-important to slow down.)

(too late to say no now)

Death's the reigning champ, the heavy-weight, master magician. Unfathomably skilled in every game, from Baccharat to Scrabble, from Settlers of Catan to Go Fish; there's no game they can be beat at. Ever watch Death play DDR? You've never seen feet so fast. Nowhere to hide when it's your time.

Death is a father walking their child down the aisle, steady. Certain. Death doesn't leave mid-way through, doesn't skip town to go be with someone else. Death is constant, sturdy. Even patient to a certain degree, but unyielding to the rules of their game.

There's no winning, but we play anyway.

There's no new victor to be crowned, but we do our best anyway.

Death is change.

Out of death and the end comes new life, a new start. We fear Death because of its predictability while missing that with it comes growth; Death is closing the chapter on what no longer serves you and cannot be saved.

III.

Dear Dead: You're Dad

father's day, 2023

unlike the spider plant, pathos, & alligator plants that came before
my grief refuses to wilt.
I shove father-figure-shaped leaves with gloved hands,
until it's backed to the edge of my mind,
a room so windowless and dark,
my thirteen-year-old self wouldn't dare come near.
I don't water it,
don't repot or fertilize.
I sure as hell don't sing to it
the way I did when my spider plant
went pale around the edges.

Still, branches grow on a steady diet of
spite and isolation,
crawling to the edges of my joy
until vines choke
the life from everything around it.

Three years I've let it lie
waiting for this to be
the year it gives up the ghost,
rotting in yellowed pieces.

Only to open the door
and face the jungle.

in which i've learned more about fatherhood from a podcast about dads than i have from my own father

or, Spotify says I've listened to over 52,000 minutes of the podcast Dungeons and Daddies in 2022

The Golden Rule has a loophole that my father never failed to exploit, as well as every man around me when they tell me how beautiful I am and how I'm such a whore for not blushing under the false weight of a compliment only given to receive something in return.

It's okay to be angry, it's not okay to be cruel, like yelling at your child when they refuse to adhere to your specific brand of reality. Like hypothesizing whether they're your child when the reality of my own anger, constant need to fight, and bullheadedness stares you back in the face.

It's not a good thing to try and be best friends with your kid. A fish raising a sea goat but only bother to see the similarities, even as the curved horns grow larger and larger every day. Still he's only focused on forcing you to swim in the same strong waters he treads every day, never realizing you need real air to breathe, need to break your head above the water from time to time. *Why are you so far behind? Keep up.*

All kids deserve knives from their daddies. I never knew guns were in the house even though there were firefights every night, verbal artillery spraying from your lips at every imagined slight. The only knives ever seen were the ones my mother threatened to take her life with.

Isn't it so valuable to have love when it's not a certainty? I wonder whether my need for love was because I never realized what it felt like when it was there. Was because the facsimile of love I witnessed was only ever a projection — hollow, superficial, unsustainable, that I thought I'd only ever find that throughout my whole life. Because how can I know what actual love looks, feels, breathes like when I've watched it tangle around my sister's legs and rip her under the water's surface?

Talking about it later doesn't mean brushing everything under the rug. When the only emotion I've seen is anger, is a plate burst like a supernova on the floor, like a room destroyed in unspoken rage, you start to think emotions have more in common with a grenade than anything else, and so are better thrown under a body, or lobbed back over enemy lines.

Holding hate in your heart doesn't make you stronger. Contrary to popular belief, spite didn't save him in the end, didn't protect him from his body breaking down, poisoned by his inability to let go of the past. Didn't restart his organs when he felt them starting to give up. How different his years could've been if he'd lightened himself of those burdens instead of forcing his back to shoulder them year after year after year.

i don't sleep with men who don't have cats

And by cats I mean boundaries.
What is a cat if not a walking, fluffy reminder
that sometimes yes means no
means i don't feel like it right now come back later
means don't fucking touch me or i bite
means if i bite you, you don't get to hit me
and pretend it meant nothing.
Means if I lash out at you
there's a reason for it.
Means look into my eyes;
see how they're scared? See how they're wide
and how my tail doesn't twitch with pleasure
but with terror?
Means don't get upset and call me a bitch
when my gaze is telling you that
if you come closer I will not hesitate to strike.
I keep my nails sharp for this reason, buck-o.
When I say I don't sleep with men who don't have cats
I mean I don't trust those who aren't bilingual,
able to speak the language of my body as well as my heart,
who don't respect the clear repercussions of fuck around and find out
without lashing out in anger themselves. Means I don't
deal with half-assed apologies and yes
I will disappear on you
if you mistreat me, will seek shelter elsewhere,
a warmer, safer bed than yours
if you neglect to recognize that your wants do not equate to mine.
Means I don't have to accept being hit
and being expected to come back for more,
or that I'll let you rub my nose into a mess I only made
to tell you you fucked up, now deal with it.

My teeth are sharp and my memory is long; I hold grudges
closer than I hold my emotions, and while I'm working on trusting
I'm also working on learning caution. Nine lives may be enough for some
but you'll find they run out quicker than expected
if you trust every Tom, Dick, or Harry that comes along.

Now. Women, on the other hand.
There's a joke to be made here
(because I am my father's daughter)
but we're in polite conversation,
so I'll just see myself out now.

do you ever think about who you'd be if you'd had a dad?

Not a man whose efforts in your conception lasted less than a dinner date.

A father. A man who knew that love didn't come with terms + conditions, as if loving you was akin to signing up for a credit card.

23.9% APR [Arguing about Parental Responsibility],
monthly charges may apply if not enough placating calls are made (to him).
Agreement subject to change depending on the day/time/holiday.
No, he's not open on holidays
(and yes banking holidays are included);
No his hours will not be flexible to accommodate
your needs; you should have thought about that before.
Good luck getting a return on that deposit of affection
when all he knows is how to
squirrel away what's given to him
so he can (maybe) find it on a rainy day.

Did you ever think about
what it might be like to find equal time parenting
wasn't about checks and balances in time
but in heart-to-heart conversations?
In moments asking *what do you think?*
Rather than *how could you be so stupid?*

Do you imagine a world where your value isn't
aligned with how many years until
you're 18. One where instead
how many times you're asked
about your failures,
you're celebrated even for
your lackluster successes?
try measuring the space in days left
when you can still be naive enough
to think that *no* doesn't have to mean *yes*
just because your boyfriend wants it
when *no* has never meant *no*
when it comes to what your father wants.

i'm what you call a lexapro girlie

Let me sing you the song of my people.
It begins with:
> *everyone you know hates you*
> *you don't actually have any friends*
> *you're so fucking annoying*

And ends with:
> *did you take your meds today?*
> *did you eat yet?*
> *when was the last time you drank water?*

You'll be singing the catchy refrain all day:
> *you aren't half as talented as you like to act.*

And it has such a killer bridge:
> *when's the last time you went to bed on time?*

If you play it on repeat you'll hear:
> *you're going to die alone, unloved, and your cats will eat your eyeballs for the moisture.*

But it's only when you play it backwards you catch:
> *shut the fuck up, dad.*

falling asleep to a podcast about horror movies

what's the point of a scary movie
when the demons
& monsters
& hell creatures
& villains
parade in the broad daylight?
(white hoods optional.)

what's the point of a horror movie
film
or story
or podcast
or show
when real life supplies enough stories to keep you listening for a lifetime?

who needs a haunted house
when i know the monster's best
hiding places?
no shadows needed, no creeping necessary;
they move slowly enough
you can see them with ease
through the hallways
of their churches
houses of government
& board rooms.

white noise feels like

slipped fingers around ribs

scratched nails on walls

while the vhs

    skips

          skips

               skips

begging for oblivion

between the lows and highs

of background noise

a place in the world

Nostalgia is when my hand soap
smells like dad's cologne, the one he wore
when we were getting ready to go out to eat
and I knew that for just one night
everything was going to be okay.

It's seeing the exact shade of pink
Grandma used to imprint on my
cheek when I came over to
dye easter eggs, the whole house smelling
like vinegar and covered
in yesterday's newspaper.

Nostalgia is the way that sometimes
really good Chinese food makes me cry,
how a mildewy basement can feel like home,
and the reason why fighting feels as intimate
and familiar as a warm hug. A time when
things were easier.

    Not better.
    Just easier.

executive dysfunction

Executive
> power suits and c-suites
> not even a boss babe
> can touch;
> my bloody nails
> barely dent the thickest
> glass ceilings.

dysfunction
> an incorrect piece;
> the system sliding
> through cracks, yet still not large enough
> to allow egress;
> a one way exit
> for the bits and pieces
> of myself to slip through.

family therapy session 4

ever strike a match and before you realize it's caught,
before heat, spark, & flame registers,
you start to bring it back to the box's edge
just to find the taste true fear leaves on your tongue?

ever think about what can happen
if you bring your hand
just a couple inches closer?

dear dead: you're dad

and we've only meet a handful of times
                    but isn't it crazy
        that everyone I work with
      says we have the same eyes?

Isn't it great
that all my best jokes
are the ones
        said in your humor?
Laughter whittled out
            like a rattle of chipped
            teeth.

I always thought you'd be a stranger;
someone I wouldn't meet
until later in my life
but whose tailcoats I'm always chasing.
Turns out you were waiting
to introduce yourself.   Tried once
      but I was too young to remember.

I'm grown now. I know now
to look for you twice before   I cross each road,
to think that every truck   that passes me
with heavy logs or machinery   might have you at the wheel.
I know the warning signs   when you're On Call,
waiting minute by minute
until I show up so   you can do your Thing.

Thanks for looking out.

i told him once he couldn't die until he walked me down the aisle.

I wonder if he gave up the day I told him I didn't believe in marriage anymore.

I'm not sure if it was relief,   or disappointment
But I remember the way his face
fell.

Why bother, I thought
What has a wedding ever done for him?

what if i get to be the villain?

Imagine the day I'm not lambasted for my every plan,
where I have henchmen who hang on
my every word as though
it's come from god herself.
Where I'm the one
with the maniacal laugh,
—I've already got it practiced, gotten so good, just you wait—
telling you that you'll never outsmart my plan—
& I'm right?
What if
I get to be the one
who walks away with the girl
at the end of the film?
& we ride off into the sunset together
with the world at my fingertips,
where the adoration I've spent so much of my life
chasing shines back at me from the seams
of the horizon.
What if
I get to be right?
or better,
what if
I get to be wrong?

reflection on "what if i get to be the villain?"

"I support women's rights but more than that I support women's wrongs." I really think that we as a society forget that as over fifty percent of the population, we get to be wrong, too.

Not wrong as in, "you dumb broad, you really thought you had the right answer" or, "you silly slut, you think you know better."

Wrong as in fuck you, I'm keying your car for cheating on me.

Wrong as in some days I would like to know what it means to sink my knuckles into the flesh of the next sonuvabitch that tells me to smile.

Wrong as in if you try to touch my ass again I'll knock you flat onto your back, and then I'll take you to court for harassment.

What does it mean for a woman to be able to be wrong, to be able to take back her own strength and channel it into something—dare I say—dastardly? What would it mean to us as a society if women were allowed to fuck up and it was laughed off as being human, rather than being another explanation for being "the weaker sex"? What would it mean if I got to shrug off my incompetencies as just being a normal person, rather than apologize and genuflect for all the ways in which I should've prepared myself better to fuck up, because we all knew it was coming after all?

More than that, what would it mean if we didn't hold women to these exacting standards and we let them be real. True. Authentic.

Why does a woman have to be a villainess, why can't she be a villain? Why does she have to be a countess, not a count? Why an actress, not an actor? Don't give me the bullshit about language; English is three misshapen languages in a jumpsuit pretending to have its shit together at morning yoga, when really it's as butchered as the slab of beef you'll serve for dinner.

When do I get to be the bad guy?

my therapist says this is profound; i say it's middle of the night shitposting.

I tried on fake nails for the first time one afternoon, bought them on a lark. 7.99 to satiate my curiosity (if only that was the cost for everything I've been curious about; I'd be a rich woman). I took them from the package, leaf-green plastic shells tumbling out like beetle carapaces, skittering into formation as I fitted the pieces to my plain nails.

Glued skin together on more than one occasion; beginner's error. Glued wrong pieces to skin and felt it pull, unmovable, when I tried to get them free. Wondered, in all seriousness, whether there'd be glue left over to patch up a relationship or to fix together two ends of a trailing argument that never got its ending.

But after the tears and the laughter at how ridiculous I must have looked with one whole set on, trying (and failing, often) to squeeze glue out of a tube intended to keep it in, I sat there and marveled at my hard work. I got it. I was Cool Girl. I was Amy Dunne, and every woman that came before and after. I was effortless and powerful, claws long enough to deal damage (super effective, critical hit sort), long enough to give the best kitty scritches.

I was unstoppable, found myself gesturing with my fingers to prove my point, my weapons already attached and ready to slice and dice and cut any rebuttal to ribbons. Cool Girl doesn't have to repeat herself when the blades on her fingertips say it all.

And then I tried typing, and all that fell away.

You know how hard it is to feel refined when you're tip-tapping at keys that your fingers know more intimately than your own body? You know how difficult it is to feel chic when you try to pull your pants up and a nail pops off, clattering to the floor like some glimmering creature just shed its skin? Can you imagine how difficult it is to feel like a Cool Girl when you're mashing the pads of your finger against a screen that once unlocked at a single glance, but now it doesn't even recognize the person you're trying to be?

I popped the nails off piece by piece, soaked my cuticles in acetone and let the facade fall into the trash can, attempts at finding a new piece of me splintering and skittering into the garbage. Stared at my still-glue covered nails and prayed for patience to keep from picking at the scab of what could've been an achievement, but was instead a reminder that y'know . . . I like my nails short.

Besides, you ever scratch yourself trying to get off with long nails? Tried to reach that spot only to find that rounded acrylic and the softest parts of you actually shouldn't meet? Tried to find a rhythm but ended up pinching and slicing at nerves in a way they never were meant to be touched? Worked to find some semblance of bliss in a world too far gone, just to discover that what you thought made you a boss babe, Cool Girl, effortless and living your best life, means reaching an orgasm becomes ten times more difficult and fifty times more hazardous?

No thanks. I'm good not being Cool enough to figure it out.

caught somewhere between terror and horror

terror is the recognition that half of your dna comes from him
horror is failing to pull him out strand by strand.

terror is seeing brown hair, dimples, and a strong chin in the mirror
horror is listening to him talk in your dreams.

terror is counting calories, food journaling, and considering maybe trying *just one* fad diet
horror is understanding no purge will ever get him out.

terror is jonesing for an argument, picking at sores and scabs until you're bloody
horror is bandaging yourself up alone, wondering when *this time* will be the *last time*.

terror is walking alone at night and hearing a second set of footsteps
horror is the uncertainty about whether your father would ever believe you.

terror is a night in the house alone
horror is knowing he'll never leave.

family therapy session 5

loving you
is pushing my tongue
to the burned roof of my mouth
and wondering why it hurts

"if there was one thing your father was good at, it was cooking."

My tastebuds come with a predetermined yearning for
Salt
    Acid
        Fat
           Sugar

My gut distends with determination to season—
and season *well*—
any food that leaves my hands
& makes it to the bellies of my loved ones.
I might be pale as an undercooked scallop
but I'll be damned if there isn't
a time I reach a spoon in to taste
& come away with a sigh
& added pinch of
salt between my fingers
lovingly sprinkled over my meal

& another
thrown over my shoulder.

reflection on "if there was one thing your father was good at, it was cooking"

My grandmother was the one who told me that, and often, especially when I'd go to her house for cooking. The woman who fed us on chicken and crunchy (read: undercooked) rice for get togethers, who was notorious for never using garlic even after her husband died because he didn't like it, who cut the mold off of cheese and offered up squares from the same block, always had something good to say about my father's cooking.

Nothing else. Just that he knew how to cook. And he did. I grew up on a steady diet of food I hated but was forced to sit at the table to finish, and food that I couldn't get enough of, a strange dichotomy of never wanting more and yet being too full to understand that I was building an unhealthy relationship with food and eating. It was a common refrain around the dinner table, that if your plate wasn't cleaned—whether you liked it or not—you weren't leaving the table.
I cried my way through mouthfuls of lima beans and brussel sprouts, through sauerkraut that to this day doesn't taste right unless it's extra salty.

Maybe that's why I'm so used to well-salted food, why a dish doesn't feel complete until I've added that last pinch. When you're force-fed a diet of tears and calories, it just doesn't taste done until you've added that final touch.

My dad used to put salt on his watermelon, on his corn on the cob, on his ice-cream; I never had the wherewithal to ask him if he'd cried through mealtimes, too.

family therapy session 6

even knowing that
drinking poison is like taking
revenge and wishing
the other person
would shrug it off, like retribution
served with a sugared rim,
crystal glass, leadened with fair play—

sometimes I just want your eye, too.

this is a love letter

mother's perfume/mary kay and hopes and dreams wrapped into weekly meetings like she's part of an anonymous group addicted to the grind/sample cosmetics stretched across my face like scars I settled on creating myself/spice girls/if you wanna be my lover/call out to the world/spice up your life/sung down country roads at six am/violin in the backseat/my sister driving to the coffee shop in town before class/driving those same roads seven years later and singing at the top of my lungs/alone/kitten purrs and biscuits made of skin and belly rubs/the way my maddie fit right in the crook of my arm/the welcoming yowls of addie-girl as I walked through the door/fall nights spent in the clutch of friends/leaning on shoulders strong enough to keep me steady/Shania Twain and karaoke in the car before the Internet came around/Y2K glasses filled with bubbly grape juice/first sips of champagne when the world didn't crash around us/the promise of freedom with a driver's license/mix tapes and mixed messages/oh those high school years/texting with one thumb on the pulse of a relationship/the other flipping pages of my planner/filled to the brim with good intentions/and high expectations/red dresses and dances with best friends/ midnight krispie kreme runs after the high from prom wore my soul to the bone/slow drives back from grandma's house/middle of the nights woken up crying/mom picking me up with a persistent apology in her eyes/"guess you're not ready for nights away from home yet"/tattered blanket that comes further and further apart with every wash/aged popcorn-butter yellow and faded design picked from overly anxious fingers/falling like snow in bed/Christmas caroling in the snow until my cheeks ache from the cold/half-birthdays and holiday mixtapes made just for mom and my drives/bootlegged movies and sneaking sister's CDs/the real slim shady and big pimpin' jay-z/pushin' it salt-n-pepa and chasing waterfalls with tlc/numb linkin park and sitting pretty fly with the offspring/bring it on and ten things I hate about you/giggling along when my sister laughs/hoping she thinks I understand the jokes/first kisses in the high school stairwell/closed eyes and sweaty palms/waiting for mom to pick me up/butterflies threatening to spill when he takes my hand/movie marathons and nights spent writing/and writing/and writing/sure to make it one day/

when do we stop counting?

Inspired by Innocent by Taylor Swift (Taylor's Version)

What is the past if not a war campaign we wage against ourselves?
Reflection and hindsight is 20-20, but what they don't tell you
is you're twenty-for-twenty
fucking up your life.

What is the past if not a shattered reflection of what we thought it might be?
the media we consumed
could never prepare us for
the pain that comes with realizing
our biggest enemies will always
be ourselves

What is the past if not backing the car out of your childhood driveway?
You're never too old to grow up and to learn
but it's hard to see your softened edges for the hard ones
when the sharpened edges cover the gentlest bits
and the rounded corners you once knew like the back of your hand
stop showing up in your rearview mirror.

What is the past if not your father's voice in your ear whispering when you
mess up?

Thirty-two now; I'll have more years spent without him
than with.

you know how i know the patriarchy has me fucked up?

Because when talking with my therapist about how fortunate I've been to never have been sexually assaulted, my first thought was: why not, though? Was I not pretty enough? Am I not desirable? Was I too confident, too loud, too Much?

While I should be grateful for my luck, my brain's first thought is: but what's wrong with me?

i started my therapy journey in 2020 and i want to get off this ride

The problem with starting therapy is that you can't unstart. Can't go back to licking your wounds in private without thinking about the hurt that caused someone to hurt you. Can't go back to ignoring your trauma, or working harder to offset the pain, without recognizing the damage you're doing; and no matter how you try to push it to the back, you know you can't.

Won't.

There's no way forward that goes around; there's only through. And through? Means you learn to love the pain, regardless of if you're ready for it or not.

Or at the very least expect it.

The problem with knowledge is there's no unknowing. There's no reset to bring you back before you knew better, only the disbelief when you do it all over again despite the warning signs. There's no going back to simpler times without understanding, and acknowledging, the regression; no matter how badly you want to forget, to be able to hold a grudge—to feel the anger, the spite, the shame overwhelm your every moment, there's a part of you that's too smart to go down that road again, that knows better than to turn left when every sign points right (especially when left guides you to the well-traveled road of your past.)

And the call for grace that sounds somewhat like your therapist when you try to be hard on yourself about it.

The real problem with therapy?

I can't be cruel to myself without recognizing my father's timbre in my voice and understanding the disappointment has never been mine to begin with. I can't be caustic to my connections without hearing my mother's own desire to push everyone away and bear the weight of the world on shoulders so strong they make Atlas jealous. I can't stop seeing every time I second guess myself as a way to protect myself from an unknowable future, and can't shut out the voice that tells me it's okay for me to try.

I can't cut off that which doesn't serve me on a whim because I woke up on the wrong side of the bed, and I can't hold my anger down deep and let spite fuel me like my grandmother before me, even though *god* it feels good to be able to say *I fucking told you so.*

I can't unhear the voices that I spent so many years thinking were my own that echo now in the chamber of my desires to do good.

And that's really fucking annoying.

fictional fathers should come with a warning.

I wept when Ned Stark died.
Found him a father figure I'd been desperate for,
needing someone to look favorably on me
to tell me that they believed in me
pointy weapons and all, and that
I could one day be great.
That even if we were to be parted for a while, we'd have
the conversation that was needed when he got
back.

I sobbed when Odin died.
Forgetful and negligent though he was,
a father he still had been;
bringing two sons into the world
where only one had been wanted.
All-father, all seeing and all knowing,
an absentee father to the boys
begging for his attention;
maybe that's why I found him so
familiar.

I cried when Mufasa died,
slipping from the edge of the cliff, betrayed
by a brother that had desires and ambitions that
he, in all his goodness, could never see,
watched him cry out to the son he'd always watched over
and felt in my heart that a father should never
put themselves in harm's way; the pain
of losing is simply too great to handle.

I screamed when Theoden died
in the arms of his niece.
Broken shield and battered honor

but brilliant and bold to the end; a soldier staring Death
in the face and daring it to move first.
Clutched in Eowyn's arms, he knew her face,
and passed his fury to her, his strength and his sword
as constant as the beating of her heart.

I trembled when my father slipped from the world
open-mouthed and gaping, gone before I was able
to hold his hand on the hospital bed,
stroking the back of his palm as he stared unseeing,
unspeaking, a stroke stealing the last of his breath
as tears crawled down the edges of my face, dripping
onto the blue-gray gown they'd dressed him in.

You'd have thought that so much death
could have prepared me for losing
a man whose shortcomings were the soil
in which my own grew.

I wish.

in the back of your head

Inspired by Spanish Sahara by Foals

The mirror's clouded with the steam from the shower, as though the heat could leech the fury from my bones as effectively it does the ache from my muscles. Standing there, towel and sweat and drip, drip, drops of water on vinyl flooring, a cat screaming at the door to be let in, I'm shapeless even to myself. Yellow toweled blur, blue painted background, I could be anyone.

Anything.

I could be happy, maybe, if I'd just let myself.

The first crack of the door welcomes in the August chilled air, the howling cat, and with both the steam begins to pull in from the edges. A bathroom pulled into focus piece by piece, fitted together to feature a disembodied, headless blur in the middle; my features, centered on the glass, are the last to gain any clarity.

I could be anyone's daughter. Anyone's mistake, their child, their supposed-to-be. I could be anything, an unhaunted form begging for shape and clarity.

I stand and watch the features of my body pull into focus, Grandma's hips and father's penchant for holding weight, stretch marks and cellulite and all shapes that rhyme with round. Mother's trauma and sister's sorrow define the set of my shoulders, the curve of my neck, the tight lump in my throat.

I breathe steam back against the mirror as my face starts to gain focus, the slice of cheeks, a chin. The starting of brown hair newly grown from being shaved. I watch the steam morph my body again, blanketing them in familiar, comfortable anonymity. I let my breath go.

And hold the steam in.

breathing 101

insane to think it's possible to make suffocating
look like an art form, yet here we are. i only learned
how to breathe in 2020. before, had made a home out of
over-inflated lungs, bedfellows with the unnamed pressure
in my chest that could've just as easily been
a heart attack, stroke, undiagnosed cancer, a panic attack,
period cramps, indigestion, depending on what
day you asked.

learned from an early age to shake this discomfort off, ignoring
false-narratives of friends who knew how oxygen
tasted. learned to apply foundation to hide blue, sickly
skin, to slick on mascara and thick eyeliner to draw
attention from bloodshot eyes, lacquered my lipstick so red it
offset the offputting color of my mouth. learned to live
a light-headed life from morning to midnight.

at 18, college living looked like
experimenting with short gasps,
growing drunk on the taste of salvation
moving to a new city brought;
stole sips of air like an alcoholic
taking communion on Sundays, snuck
benediction wherever I could find it.

it wasn't until I held my father's
limp hand, his mouth open in one final breath,
flinty eyes unseeing,
I found the strength to exhale
hard enough that the weight of another man's world
finally rolled off my shoulders.

Acknowledgements

Gracious, where do I begin?

This book felt like tapping into a vein and watching the past thirty-plus years spill out: the good, the bad, the very bad, the day to day, and the (what I thought maybe?) profound. But this would not have been started or even considered if not for my therapist and Melissa for urging me to write down my thoughts, to begin a collection of essays and poems and ramblings about my *feelings*, about how I felt while working through everything the last few years. Chérie, Mel, thank you both from the absolute bottom of my heart.

Emily and Jessica, thank you for being there throughout the last few years especially. For having my back, being my anchors, for believing in me that I can do the hard things, even the ones I don't think I want to do but know I have to.

Huge shout out to my mother, to my bonus-dad Dan for believing that I could write something and trusting I knew what I was doing. Thank you both for your constant support, for picking me up when I had my first major panic attack so I wouldn't die alone, as I was convinced I would.

Thank you Genna for reading the brief snippets I sent over Snapchat and telling me that they were actually worthwhile. Thank you for being proud of me, just as I am so, so proud of you.

Thank you to Sarah, for your eagle eyes, for the edits that made this book what it is. Thank you for calming my anxiety and my fear that this wasn't anything other than a Mess and for your guidance getting it to where it is now. You're incredible.

Thank you to Poet for the stunning artwork on the cover! For letting me send you my stick-drawing and panicked last minute ideas of what I wanted the cover to look like. Thank you for your kind heart and for being an incredible friend through it all.

To Becca, my darling dearest. I hope this helps you find some peace going through your loss. To Molly, Marc, Faith, Puzz, Chris, Dina, Angela, Ari, Stephanie, Vee, Megan, Bun, and I know I'm forgetting others so I hope you will forgive me. Thank you for BELIEVING in me, for your kindness and grace, for your friendship and love. Marc, I couldn't have typeset and created the cover for this without you, you rockstar. Thanks for always believing in me.

Thank you to Sophie and Pippa, whose likeness makes up Two Small Smudges, for your (mostly) unconditional love . . . unless treats are involved. Thank you for keeping me sleep deprived so I can get the emotions out when they need to, and for never failing to keep me humble when I mess up and y'all give me the BIGGEST side eye. Especially you, Sophie.

For Maria, I miss you every damn day. I hope you know you're so loved. For Addie and Maddie, thank you for teaching me how to love without limits.

Grandma Bernadine, I can still hear you say, "Oh, Audrey. Isn't that something?" I hope you would think this is, indeed, something.

And for Dad . . . I've said all there is to say, I think. For better or for worse, I'm pretty sure I know what you'd say. I'll let myself pretend it's positive.
Today would've been your 74th birthday.

Of course, shout out to Taylor Swift & Billie Eilish, who'll never read this, but they got me through my absolute saddest of days, and beyond. Soundtracks to write to, I swear.

To the podcast Dungeons & Daddies (not a BDSM podcast) which saw me through the loss of my father, and provided me therapy before I was ready to actually *go* to therapy.

And to you, dear reader, holding this in your hand, on your eReader, or however you got a copy of this. **Thank you**. Thank you for witnessing me, and please know that you are not ever alone, no matter what you're going through.

If you resonated with this book of poems, essays, and reflections in any way, consider leaving a review on Goodreads, Amazon, or wherever you review books; knowing that my work struck a chord with someone, or was relatable, is truly the most rewarding part of the writing process.

Growing up, Audrey Jean (she/her) knew she was going to be an author one day, she just wasn't sure how. Or when. Let alone of what. But there was always something to say, and she was keen to find a way to say it. Her next book, which she hopes won't be as depressing as this one, is planned for a 2025 release, and will be her first foray into fiction (and romance!). When she's not writing something or other, you can usually find her trying to make a dent in her ever-growing TBR pile, working on training her cats to take walks, or stewing over a new cookbook with flour inevitably streaked over her front.

If that doesn't work, look in the mirror, spin around twice while saying, "Do you want to watch the 2005 version of Pride and Prejudice?" and she'll show up behind you with a bottle of wine, ready to go.

If you're interested in connecting and seeing what's coming next, you can find her at: **audreyjean.net | Instagram: audreyjean_writes | Patreon: audreyjean**